I Survived

I Survived

A Murder Untold

Myra C. Fox

Copyright © 2008 by Myra C. Fox.

ISBN: Hardcover   978-1-4363-6943-5
       Softcover   978-1-4363-6942-8

All rights reserved. No part of this book may be reproduced or transmitted in any form or by any means, electronic or mechanical, including photocopying, recording, or by any information storage and retrieval system, without permission in writing from the copyright owner.

This book was printed in the United States of America.

To order additional copies of this book, contact:
Xlibris Corporation
1-888-795-4274
www.Xlibris.com
Orders@Xlibris.com
53033

Contents

Chapter 1　My Childhood Days 11

Chapter 2　A Long Walk 18

Chapter 3　The Babysitter 22

Chapter 4　The house and the Tragedies 26

Chapter 5　The Other Room, the Pig and the Garden 31

Chapter 6　When We Ran Away 38

Chapter 7　Her Last Breath 44

Chapter 8　The Murder Untold 47

Chapter 9　I Survived 49

Author's Note 69

This Is Dedicated To The One I Love 71

"Here is what I survived through the grace of God and

here is the murder and here is the untold"

DEDICATION

First and foremost to God, who is the reason why I am here to tell this story.

To: My Pastor and First lady, Bishop and Edith Faison whom I know love me.

To: My Church Family at Church Of God and True Holiness Fredericksburg, who prays for me.

To: Pastor Lynn Beanum and wife, Ruby Beanum and daughter, Tracey Carter. For all your support in a difficult time. I love you.

To: The Church at 522 Louisa, Virginia. Thanks for everything you did.

To: Dr. Gayle Wolfe who gave me the psychological guidance to start the book.

To: My daughter LaSonja who sat up with me night after night until I finished this book. I Love You.

To: My oldest daughter, Shereica who helped research and gather information that I thought was impossible. I Love You.

To: My grandchildren, Mypri and Castle who always have their grandmother's back. I Love You.

To: A good friend, Estelle Samuels who believed in me and her daughter Teresa who I know if no one else reads this book, she will.

To: Nikkie and Katrina Booker thanks for giving me a start I never thought I would get. Never forget how much I Love You.

To: My mom Mary, who has always been there.

To: My sister Requal, for her love and support.

To: Octavia Shields, for your support and wisdom.

To: Cathy Adams, a very special friend who has supported me through difficulties in my life.

To: Bishop Pratt and his Wife Hannah Pratt who have always believed in me.

To: Bennie Evans, a great friend and a great person.

To: Faye Campbell and family, I Love You.

To: My biological family, Washington D.C.

To: Dr. Bernstein*, Dr. Lisa King*, Dr. Donato*.

To: My Pendleton family, the late Paul Pendleton Sr. and wife; (Jeff, Nikki, Paul Jr., Kenny, Samantha, Melissa, Jr., Jerome)

To: James Willis who kept me going. Frank Perez*, Calvin Jay*, Robert Fox*, Daniel Smith*(Son-in-law), Ron Trotter*

And to all that I didn't mention, I love you and God Bless . . . .

Chapter 1

My Childhood Days

THIS STORY IS so deserving of so many titles, it was very hard to pick a title befitting of this story. I am taking this Story back to when I was a little girl around nine or ten years of age living in Washington D.C. I want to tell you of some of the tragic events that happened in my life while living there.

I want to tell you how I survived the things that no little girl that age should ever have went through. I want to also tell you of a tragic murder that took place after I was taken from Washington D.C. and brought to Virginia. It is a miracle that I have lived to tell this story.

There were five of us; I had two brothers and two sisters. My mother always thought a lot of her boys and not so much of her girls. We were all shipped around a lot, the girls more than the boys. We didn't really stay in one place for more then a few months so we didn't go to school very much at all, except for Huck. He was the oldest of all; he lived with my mother's grandmother. His life was a lot different from the rest of us.

He always lived with my great grandmother, we never saw him much at all except maybe when our mother would take us all to Silver Spring, M.D. to see our great grandmother. I remember when we went to see her, we could only go into one room in her house and that was the kitchen where we sat around the kitchen table. It seemed like as soon as we got there we had to eat and then we were getting our things together to leave.

She always wanted us to hurry up and leave, I remember her always saying "Hurry up and get your things together so when your mother comes back you can go, I wish she had never brought you here and left you." I never understood why she always said that, because we never did anything but sit at the kitchen table.

Denise was the next oldest; she was tall and had the prettiest hair, it was so long and kind of curly I loved my big sister but she was not nice to us all the time, only when we had something she wanted. I was next, I had sandy red hair it was a little shorter then Denise's and everyone called me "Robin" but my name was Myra. Castle was after me, she had cold black wavy hair, it was very long and the color of her skin was very dark, but not so dark that you couldn't see a black mole on her left cheek.

She was so pretty to me, she never said much but when she did talk she talked about God and about loving people. When she would get a beating you could hardly hear her cry. I remember when I would get a beating or she saw me crying she would always put her arms around me and tell me not to cry, that it would be okay. I always lay in her lap and it made me feel better. Tyrone was the baby of all. He was so skinny and he too was very dark, we all looked after him.

When my mother would come to pick us up she always complained to our great-grandmother that she couldn't find a place to live and that she needed money. My grandmother would always give her money to help with finding a place for us to stay. She always told our mother to make sure she got us something to eat, but as soon as we left she would go by a store and buy cigarettes, beer or liquor. When we did find a place to stay it was always a very bad and scary place, and we only stayed a few months, I remember one of the places we lived was on 16th Street in Washington D.C. the reason I remember it so well is because there was a store front across from the apartment building where we were living and it had cookies, three for a penny.

Every time I found a penny I would rush across the street and give the man my penny for three cookies. I always saved one for Castle and a little piece for Tyrone, I would hurry and eat mine and hide the rest for Castle and Tyrone because Denise would always take all of the cookies if she knew I had them. I think we all felt very protective of Tyrone because he was so skinny. Not that we weren't, but we were just left alone so much that we felt the little one had to be safe.

I remember this one night we were staying in this apartment building, I think we were on the 4th floor but there were so many more floors further up. Well this one night we were left alone; my mother was not around only Denise, me, Castle and Tyrone. I heard a loud noise outside our door so I pulled a

I SURVIVED

stool up so that I could see out of the peep hole. When I looked out, I saw this tall man in a black suit and with a big hat walking pass the door. He was going up the next set of steps where my mother's friend Miss. Jean lived.

I heard him stop at her door and knock, then all I heard was screaming. I knew it was Miss. Jean who was screaming, and then I heard a gun shot. I remember that I got so scared I ran into my mother's room and got behind the door. The edge of the door hit the end of her dresser so that it made a little hole where you could hide behind the door in.

No one could see me so I got behind it and stooped down, I heard Tyrone crying. He was at the foot of the bed. I yanked him to me and hid him with me behind the door. I told him to be quite and to close his eyes. I didn't know where Castle and Denise were; I just felt like I had to protect Tyrone. I had to keep him safe. A few minutes later a knock came at the door and it was the police they kept saying "open the door it's the police." I held on tight to Tyrone and stayed behind the door, my sister Denise went to the door and opened it. The police came in. They asked was my mother home Denise told him no the police asked was there anyone else in the house, I heard my sister say "No."

I remember hearing the police walk around the house. They asked my sister where my mother was. She said she didn't know. They never came to the bedroom where I and Tyrone were. Then I heard them say "Stay in the house and don't open the door for no one except your mother, do you understand me?" My sister said okay and then they left.

I heard the police go upstairs and then run back down, not long after that my mother came home and got us and went straight upstairs to Miss. Jean's apartment. My mother went over to the window, I went with her. When we looked out, down on the sidewalk we saw Miss. Jean sitting there screaming. She was screaming "He made me jump, he made me jump."

Her legs were curled up under her and she kept saying that she couldn't walk and that her legs were broken. My mother told us to go back to the apartment and stay there while she went down to see about Miss. Jean. When she came back she told us that this man in a black suit and hat held a gun on Miss. Jean and told her to jump out of the window. She said that she had to jump or he was going to shoot her.

We moved not long after that to another apartment building and not long after we moved the lady named Miss. Jean started living upstairs from us it was the last floor in the building. She never came down because she had a cast on her leg and she couldn't walk very well. I remember one day my mother sent me up to carry Miss. Jean something, I loved playing on the banisters I always lay backwards over the banisters it was fun. So this day, I was waiting for Ms. Jean to come to the door; I was playing around and lying backwards over the banisters. All I remember after that was waking up in the hospital.

My mother was sitting beside me when I woke up, I heard the doctor say that I had been asleep for two days and that I would never get my teeth back. My mother told me later that I had fallen over the banisters and that each section broke my fall and that is why I was alive. She also said that every time the doctor told me to spit because of all the blood in my mouth, I would spit out teeth. I don't remember the fall and I don't remember any pain.

When I came home from the hospital it wasn't long after that we moved again, this time it was to a house on 12th street. It looked rotten on the outside but it was kind of okay on the inside. On the corner was a store. I was glad because I didn't have to go far when my mother would send me to get something from the store. There was also an apartment building next to the store. I remember playing in front of it a lot.

There was a man that always stood on the front steps of the apartment building. He would say hi to all the little children. We all thought he was so nice. He would sometimes call us to him and give us a lollipop or some kind of candy. One day I went to the store for my mother and I saw him standing on the steps. It was raining that day, I waved but he didn't wave back. he just kept his head down when I came out of the store he was still standing there so I walked over to him to say hi and to ask for a piece of candy.

I remember he just looked at me and then he asked me if I really wanted a piece of candy. I said yes, He said that the candy was in his room and that he had to go get it, I said okay and stood there. Then he said I could come with him to his apartment where I could get a lot of candy. So, I started to follow him down the hallway. It was a long hall, as I was following behind him he reached into his pocket and held his hand down beside him I looked down and saw a knife I walked just a few more steps and turned and ran out of the building.

I ran home. I didn't tell anyone, but I never wanted to go to the corner store anymore, but I knew I would have to because my mother would send me. One day, she told me to go to the corner store for her I couldn't say no I just had to go, when I got outside some kids were walking that way so I joined the group when we got there, I looked at the apartment building where the man was always standing and he wasn't there. I went in the store and came out-he was still not there, I was sent to the store many times and I always looked to see if he was standing on the front steps but I never saw him again.

The house where we were staying was kind of big and I liked it because it had a upstairs where I liked to play and hide, I remember doing a really bad thing when we lived there, I am about to tell you something that my mother and no one ever knew. They never found out about what I did and how this time it was my fault, we had no place to stay. I have never forgiven myself until now. One day my mother had some company over. She was having a little party. My sisters and brother were outside playing I was outside too; but I wanted to go inside and play upstairs. So I left my sisters and brother outside and went into the house to play. To this day I have always wished I hadn't gone in the house. I wish I had stayed outside as I was told.

I went inside and heard my mother and her friends in the back of the house. So I went upstairs to hide and play around. I saw that there were some matches on the stand beside my mother's bed; I picked them up and tried to strike one. It lit up so I kept on striking them. I was afraid that someone might catch me so I crawled under my mother's bed and kept lighting the matches, as I was striking them the mattress started to burn. I climbed out from under the bed and ran downstairs into the living room and sat on the couch like I was there all the time.

I didn't know what to do so I just sat there, then my mother came out of the kitchen to the living room, she saw me and asked me what I was doing just sitting there, I didn't no what to say, so I didn't say anything. Then she asked me why I was not outside playing with the other children, I don't recall what I said to that, but she said it was okay and that I could stay inside if I wanted too.

My mother was sometimes was nice to us, but only when she was drinking. My mother did a lot of drinking liquor, when she drank she would treat us different. It seemed she was nicer to us when she got this way, I tried to stay away from her when she drank because she would sometimes get to falling around and call me to her and throw me down and lay on my head. I would squirm and try to yell because I couldn't breathe I always thought I was going to die. It was such a bad feeling; I would choke a lot when she let me up. This one day she was trying to be nice to me. Maybe it was the liquor and maybe because her friends were in the kitchen. So when she went back in the kitchen with her friends I sat there for a while thinking that everything was okay; then this man came running from across the street yelling that the house was on fire.

By now smoke was coming down the steps and filling the house. My mother and her friends came running out of the back of the house grabbed me and ran out the front door. Someone must have called the fire department because I could hear them far away. When they got there they ran in and started knocking down a lot of stuff. It was a long time that we stayed outside and watched, when they had finished, they came out and talked to my mother, they told her that we could not go back in the house because everything was gone that they couldn't save anything. He asked my mother did she smoke, she said yes. He asked her had she been upstairs smoking that day, she said no that she had been downstairs with her friends.

He asked her did she see anyone go upstairs or did she think one of the children had been playing with matches, my mother said no that we had been outside most of the day and that I had been sitting in the living room all day. I remember being very sorry what I had done. I have kept this to myself all this time, but I have always asked God to forgive me. I remember the fireman saying to my mother that he didn't know what happened but the mattress in her bedroom was burned so badly that nothing was left of it or anything else in the house.

To this day I don't think I have forgiven myself enough for what I did, but I think now I will start to heal. We went to stay with one of my mother's friends for a while until we could find another place. Her friend was kind of a fat man his name was Jessie. His address was so easy to remember because he lived at 1313 and 13th street, we loved it at his house it was so nice. When we had to leave Jessie's house because my mother found another place for us to live, I remember feeling very sad, Jessie's place was safe and it wasn't scary and we had plenty of food to eat. It was just so nice to live at his house, nothing bad happened while we were there except . . . . This one day I fell while I was running and playing with my sisters and brother. I fell down some steps and hit my chin on the concrete I remember there was so much blood everywhere, Jessie came running and picked me up and tried to stop the bleeding. It took so long to stop the bleeding but it finally stopped, when my mother came in he told her what had happened and that I might need to go the hospital and get some stitches. She just lifted up my chin and looked at it and said "she doesn't need to go anywhere" and then she dropped my chin out of her hand and walked away.

I grabbed my chin in my hand because the way she let it go it hurt, I remember trying not to cry, I still have that mark on my chin and if I frown you can still see the scar and the deepness of it. My mother was not a very nice person it seemed like at this time in her life and it seemed like I was the target for everything that happened and everything that was going to happen, she was always asking me to do things that were very scary.

Chapter 2

A Long Walk

THERE WAS ONE night I remember, she called me in her bedroom and told me she wanted me to go to the market for her. I cut my eyes toward the window. It was dark outside and I didn't want to go but I could never tell her that, I was afraid of what I would suffer from her hands. It would not have been good for me so I just said nothing and waited for instructions on what she wanted.

I already knew what she was sending me out for, you see. My mother would eat a lot of Argo Starch, she ate it everyday. I remember it came in a red box and a blue box. She always says if you don't see the red box get the blue box. I remember this particular night; it must have been very cold because I put on my little fuzzy red hat and a white sweater. I didn't have a coat all I had was the hat and the sweater and no matter how cold it was this was what I had to wear. I thought to my self when I get outside maybe if I ran real fast I wouldn't get to cold. My mother had given me a $1.00. She said to me in a very angry way that I should bring back her change and that it better be the right change not a penny short and that if was I wouldn't be able to sit down when I got back.

I got myself together and started out to the market which was right far away at least I thought so, but to my mother it was only a few blocks. When I got outside I thought maybe I would just walk real fast instead of running, I really don't know why I decided to do that—I just did. I had walked about two or so blocks when I notice this car following real slow behind me the car would come up close behind me and then drop back I remember feeling very afraid so I picked up my pace.

I started to walk even faster, I knew that I would soon get to a corner where I could take off running but the car picked up pace also. I looked ahead of me I could see the corner, but just as I thought I could take off running the car pulled up beside me real fast and told me to stop. I froze in my tracks. I felt so scared I just stood there. The man in the car bent down from his side of the car, looking out of the passenger's side at me he told me to come closer to the car. I just stood there. He then said to me that if I didn't come closer he would get out and put me in the car, so I moved closer to the car. He told me to bend down so that he could see me. I started to cry and hold myself, but I did as he said, I was so scared. He grabbed himself in his private area and asked me if I knew what sex was. Terrified, I shook my head no. He then said that he needed some and that I should give it to him. All I remember is that I took off running.

I could see the corner up ahead of me. I was thinking, God please just get me to the corner please get me to the corner. When I got to the corner I turned and ducked into an apartment building entrance way and stood real close up against the wall. I saw the car as it passed by where I was hiding. I thought about leaving and running to the market but I couldn't move I was just too afraid.

I stayed there I remember for a good while until I thought it was safe enough to get to the market but as I started to stepped down I saw lights of a car and stepped back into the apartment entrance way, as the car passed I saw that it was the same car and man that had stopped me earlier. I became more afraid because I thought he would be looking for me everywhere, so I stayed there a little longer. I started to worry about getting to the market for my mother's Argo starch and that I probably would get a beating for being so long. When I didn't see any cars or lights from cars come by. I took off running to the market.

I felt by now that the market might be closed, but I kept on running to get to the market all I could think of was "I hope that the man in the car was not somewhere behind me" and what was going to happen to me when I get home for taking so long and if I came back without the Argo starch and what I would say the reason was why I didn't get it." I knew I couldn't tell my mother what had happen to me because she would just say I was lying. When I got to the market it was still open I was so glad, *I* got the starch that my mother wanted and took off and started running to get home, at the same time looking back to make sure that the man in the car was not following behind me.

I remember falling down and dropping everything I had in my hand I dropped the bag and the change that the store man had given me, I picked up everything and ran even faster thinking that the man in the car might be behind me somewhere, I clutched my hands tightly around the bag and change in my hands so I wouldn't drop it again. When I got to the steps of the apartment building I was so tired but so glad to be back safe. I didn't look back I just kept straight up the steps. I stopped before I went into the house so I could catch my breath I was shaking all over I think it was from the cold and from what I had been through with the man in the car, I ran in and gave my mother the bag and I handed her the change. She never looked; she never even asked me what took me so long. I think I really wanted her to ask me so I could tell her what had happened and just maybe she might put her arms around me and hug me like I had seen people do their children on T.V. but she just grabbed the bag and change. I didn't care.

I was just glad to be in the house and safe. I started to leave the room when she said wait a minute there is some money missing. She kept counting it and counting it over and over again, I just stood there, I dare not move, when she had finished she looked at me and shouted "a penny is missing". I said I was running I must have dropped it. She barked,

"That's what you get for running you stupid child, now get back out there and don't come back until you find it because you must have spent it on candy or something, I can't send you nowhere. "She yelled at me so bad I started to cry. She said she didn't care about my crying just get out there and find it. I didn't want to go back out there I thought that the man in the car would see me again and might do something to me. I told her I was scared. She said she didn't care and that I better go so I put back on my hat and sweater and went outside.

I started crying when I got outside because I was thinking of where I must have dropped the money which to me was a long ways; I was thinking that I might see that man in the car again. I remember praying to the Lord and asking him to help me, I walked for a bit looking down the whole time I don't know if it was my praying or not but I found a penny on the ground and it was nowhere near where I had fell and dropped everything, but I was very happy at this point. I was so glad it was close to home, I ran in and gave my mother the penny. She looked at me and then she smacked my face so hard that I fell. She said the next time she sends me somewhere and I try to steal her change she would kill me.

My punishment was no dinner, and not having any dinner was nothing new to me. We never had much to eat anyway; all I wanted was to just lay down and go to sleep. I was so tired from all I had been through I didn't care if I ate or not. I crawled into bed with my sister Castle and thought about how safe I felt. I thought how I could never tell a soul about what happened to me because who would believe me if my mother didn't.

Chapter 3

The Babysitter

I REMEMBER MY mother use to leave us with this lady named Eunice Kidd, she would leave us with her very often, when we would be left with her a lot of things would happen to us that we were not allowed to tell. We kept a lot that happened to us a secret. Mrs. Kidd was also one that wouldn't feed us and would use that as a punishment, she also had a dog his name was Skippy. He was a black and white dog I remember she said he was a Cocker-Spaniel; he was not a very nice dog. He would bite us every time we got a beating from Ms. Kidd. That was one of the worse pains ever, and you couldn't get away from him. All we could do was scream and yell that we were sorry and whatever we did it wouldn't happen again just make him stop. When the beatings would stop, the dog would stop. Our skin would be torn and swollen and sometimes bleeding, we were left with all kinds of bites, bruises and marks on our bodies. Mrs. Kidd told us that this was Skippy's way of beating us for being bad.

We underwent all different kinds of abuse from Mrs. Kidd. One kind of abuse that I hated was when she would have men over almost every night some of them we would see often, and some we didn't know. I hated those times, I remember when they came to see her, we had to make food and drinks for them. It was a punishment by itself because we would be hungry but was not allowed to eat anything. we had to serve the both of them, and after they ate they would go to her bedroom and fall asleep for a while, sometimes in the middle of the night Mrs. Kidd would come to my room and tell me to get up and come to her room. I would do as I was told and when I got to her room she would tell me to sit in this chair, it was a wooden chair with a hard straw bottom, it sat across from the bed they slept in. The man would get up and bring a rope with him, he would then tie me to the chair with my arms and hands around the back of the chair then I was told to sit there and watch what they were doing boy I hated this.

I remember seeing them kiss a lot and touch a lot. He would kiss her all over, when there was something I just didn't want to see I would drop my head. When they saw that my head was down and I wasn't looking at them the man, most of the time would come over to me and smack me across the face, sometimes Mrs. Kidd would do it, one time they hit me so hard that me and the whole chair fell hard to the floor, It was so hard to sit there and watch what they did. I remember on a couple of those times when I was tied to the chair, the man would come over to me and start kissing me on my neck and rubbing his private parts. He would go down into my night pants and put his hand up in me, until it hurt me I would ask him to stop but he would tie my mouth up and keep doing what he wanted to me.

He would take his private parts and rub it all over my face he would then pull on my hair and hold my head back while he put his private part in my mouth, I remember gagging and throwing up all over myself. I was made to sit there all night tied to that chair with puke all over me sometimes he would do this more then once and she never said a word or tried to stop him. She just sat there and watched him hurt me. She didn't care at all about what was happening to me, she just let it happen. After he finished he would go back to bed with her and go to sleep. In the morning, when they would wake up they would untie me and tell me to go and get cleaned up. They said to me if I told anyone what had happened in that room that I would get a very bad beating and would be punished for a very long time. So my lips were sealed, but the memory still lingers on in my mind.

One day my mother dropped me and my sister Castle off at Mrs. Kidd's house for her to babysit us for the day; at least that is what she said when she dropped us off. I was very concerned as to why it was just Castle and me that had to go to Mrs. Kidd's that day, we all always went to her house together never split up. I wondered why Tyrone and Denise were not with us. When we got there, my mother dropped us off at the steps and said that she would be back later. It was a very strange day, Mrs. Kidd was so nice that day I remember she fed us really good and combed our hair, later a knock came at the door. A tall lady very dark and a boy came in. Mrs. Kidd talked with them in a very low voice and after a little while the lady left but the boy stayed, Mrs. Kidd told us that the boy was her nephew and that his name was Arthur. He had come to stay with her for a while and for us to go and play with him.

We played a lot that day but we also got smacked a lot after Arthur came because he would tell things on us that just weren't true, he would say that we hit him when we didn't. I remember we were always getting smacked for what we didn't do. Later that day my mother came back but when she came back she had a white man with her. He wore a short grey jacket that zipped up. He had a white shirt underneath the jacket. I looked for my sister and brother but they were not with her.

I remember we all sat down at the kitchen table Castle and I on one side my mother at the end of the table, Mrs. Kidd and the man sat across from me and Castle and Arthur was off playing in the corner next to the stove. I remember this man had a paper in his hand; he laid it on the table. He gave an ink pen to my mother and she signed the paper then he turned to Mrs. Kidd and gave her the pen and she signed the paper then they all got up from the table and shook hands. My mom just walked out with the man, I never saw my mother again after that day nor did I see my sister and baby brother.

After my mother and the man left Mrs. Kidd called me and Castle to her and put her arms around us and asked if we liked her. I remember we said yes, she then said to us that she was our mother now and that we should call her mama. She also said that we would be going on a long trip for a very long time. I remember Castle and I started to cry we told her we wanted our mother, she just kept saying that she was our mother now and to shut up. She put us into a room and locked the door; I remember the room was very small we couldn't do anything but stand up against some shelves.

I remember we were there for a long time when she let us out I had messed all over myself and Castle too, she took off our clothes and put them in a bag then took a belt and made us lie down on the floor while she beat us over and over again for messing all over ourselves she didn't even give us time to wash off she just beat us until she was tired and so did Skippy the dog. The next few days or weeks I don't remember which we just put a lot of things in boxes, I kept looking for my mother and my sister and brother, I wanted to see them. I missed my sister and brother but I never saw them again.

The next thing that happened was the man that had come with my mother that had the papers my mother and Mrs. Kidd had signed was back at the door, this time he didn't have any papers with him he said he was there to take us on the long trip that Mrs. Kidd was talking about. We all started to take boxes out of the apartment, after a while they told me and Castle and Arthur to go outside and get into the car. I don't remember being in many cars because we always went by bus everywhere. I was young but I knew how to take a bus anywhere in D.C. I needed to go. My mother had taught us this because she was always sending us to do things for her so we knew how to transfer from one bus to another.

I was only around nine years old or so but I knew my way around. I remember being very excited to be riding in a car. When we got down the steps the car was parked in front of the door, it was a long greenish and tan color car. I remember thinking it was ugly. She told us to get in the back seat and shut up and not to say anything while we were on the trip. I remember the white man getting in on the drivers side and Mrs. Kidd got in on the other side and slid real close to the white man and Skippy the dog sat next to her. The car was so big I could hardly see out of the window.

I remember trying to sit up as far as I could so that I could see out of the window but not so that Mrs. Kidd could see me. The trip seemed so long, we kept going and going on this long road that looked like it would never come to an end, we just kept going, we never turned we just kept straight I remember feeling so hungry and thirsty I wanted something to drink so bad. I remember looking over at my sister Castle she was sleeping and so was Arthur they both had been asleep for a while. I must have fell asleep also, because the next words I heard were "You can go straight into the building or you can turn left or right."

I sat up in the car and looked ahead of me. I saw the biggest white building in front of the car and it had a red flag hanging from it. She was right . . . . you could only go left or right. I think we turned left, we drove a while then we turned right and then we just kept going down another very long road and then another they were very scary and it had started to get dark the roads became even scarier, by now Castle and Arthur were awake and we were hungry. Arthur started with hitting on me and saying that I had hit him, but we were not allowed to hit him back.

Chapter 4

The house and the Tragedies

WE TURNED OFF on to this one road that was very bumpy it had a lot of dirt and rocks on it when I would look out of the window all I could see were trees and these tall poles, it was so scary I remember sliding down in my seat so I couldn't see out the window, I looked at my sister Castle she was just sitting there I thought to myself that it must be ok because she didn't seem scared at all.

The car started to slow down and then it stopped when we stopped we were in front of a white church, it wasn't very big, but it looked scary. Mrs. Kidd told us that if we didn't keep quite that a half horse half man stayed behind the church and it would come out and get us and that it only got little children.

Then she told us to get out and use the bathroom near the trees that sat on the other side of the car, Castle got out and grabbed my hand, we walked over to the woods to use the bathroom, Arthur went the other way I was so scared I kept looking for the half horse half man, we hurried and squatted down and pulled our clothes up and ran back to the car, when we got back I heard the white man say that we had broken down and that he had to get out to see what was wrong, Mrs. Kidd became very angry and started yelling some very bad words really loud, I don't really no what happened after that I just know we stayed there all night. I remember getting cold my toes felt like I couldn't move them I just laid on Castle she put her arms around me I think we both just tried to be warm, we must have all fallen asleep because I remember waking up and looking out of the window and thinking things didn't look that scary anymore because I could see everything because it was day now.

The white man got out of the car and did something under the hood for a while and then got back in and the car started up. As we drove down this bumpy dirt road we saw nothing but trees, it was like the road started to get smaller and smaller and I started to wonder more and more where we were going. We traveled a good ways down that road and finally we came to this turn on the left side of the road we turned onto it, this road was even smaller than the one we were just on, and it had a lot of holes in it, we kept down this road for a while but not to long, we came to a big yard with a big tree in it, as I looked out into the yard I saw a small house to the left it was just boards you could see straight through to the other side out into the woods, but to the right there was a door and two steps and a window the steps were not attached to the house they kind of set out from the house, Mrs. Kidd started to jump up and down she was yelling that this was her dream house and that we were going to be happy here.

I looked again at the house, the boards on the house were dark black and they looked rotten the window only had two window panes in it and I began to wonder how we would get up the steps to get into the house because the steps like I said, set out from the house and the leap to the foundation was right far to get up to.

Mrs. Kidd got out of the car and ran to the house the white man did too, they both looked at the house as if it was the best thing ever, he lifted her up to get in the house and then he jumped up to get in, we were left in the car. After a long time she came out of the house to the car and told us to get out and come to the house. As we walked to the house I felt the sun on my back it wasn't so cold now, that was nice. As we approached the house I wondered how we would get up the steps to get into the house. When we got to the steps the white man put his hand out for Mrs. Kidd when she was safe he then put his hand out for us. Arthur was the first one up he was always first, I was next and Castle was last.

When I got inside of the house I stood off to the side and looked around, what I saw was very scary, in the corner of the unfinished part of the house near the base of the ceiling was big long black thing I knew it was a snake because I had seen one in a book I yelled out and pointed it out to Mrs. Kidd and the man, there was another door off to the right of us Mrs. Kidd spoke up and told us not to worry about the snake that he live there and that he was her friend and that he wouldn't bother us if we didn't bother him, so I ran in the house, when I got inside what I saw was a long green couch under the window, in a far off corner was a single bed with a table beside it, at the door as you entered the room was a black stove with a pipe running up into the wall smoke was coming out of it.

As I looked around the room I saw another room to the left she told Castle and me to go to that room and for Arthur to stay where he was. Castle grabbed my hand and we went into the other room as we looked around the room we saw a window it had a lot of soap lined across the window seal, in the corner of the room was a single bed it had a light green cover over it, off to the left of the room was another door it had a lock on it, we just looked at the door and sat on the bed, I don't think we wanted to know what was behind it.

We heard Mrs. Kidd and the white man talking I heard him say to her that he was leaving and going home, Castle and I looked at each other I am sure we were thinking the same thing, that he had a long way to drive back to Washington D.C. we heard the door shut we just sat there on the bed Mrs. Kidd came in after a little while and told us to hold our hands out, she gave us some cold potatoes in our hand and a piece of bread I think the potatoes had been fried, I was so hungry that I just ate them up so fast and the bread too, when I looked at Castle she had only eaten a little bit of hers she asked me if I wanted some of hers she was always sharing everything she had with me I remember I said no and sat back on the bed, when I looked again hers was all gone I am sure that at first she was trying to save me some of her food to make sure I was not still hungry, she was always like that she always looked out for me even though I was older, Mrs. Kidd had Arthur bring us some water I remember when he came into the room he began to tease us saying that he had more than we had to eat.

He told us that he had chicken or something like that, he just kept laughing at us and teasing us about all the good things he had to eat he didn't realize that what we had was better than not having anything at all, even the water was good we may have been young but we had learned at a earlier age that you eat what was put before you or you didn't eat at all and we always thanked God for everything, how we knew about God I will never know we just knew he was always looking over us and that he would help us.

Maybe we knew of him from when we went to our grandmother's house, she would sometimes teach us our prayers as we sat at the kitchen table and waited for our mother to come back to get us, so when ever we got food we were grateful. When Arthur would leave the room we were glad, he was always telling lies on us and Mrs. Kidd would believe him. I remember laying down I don't know if I was tired or sick I just wanted to lay down, Castle sit back on the bed at the foot I curled up at the top, it wasn't long that we were laying there when I heard the voice of the white man he had come back I thought "How did he get back so fast?" Later when we were allowed out of the room we went into the room where they were, Mrs. Kidd told us to sit in a chair she had put next to the stove.

When we sat down I saw a pan on the stove it had a lot of potatoes in it and some chicken and some squash it looked so good I wanted some more to eat I wanted to grab some with my hands and just put it to my mouth and eat it, I remember she came over to the stove with a white plate and a fork, she put some food on the plate and carried it over to the table beside her bed where the man was sitting and put it in front of him.

She gave him something to drink she went over and sat next to him, while I was sitting next to the stove I reached up with my finger and dipped in the potatoes and put them in my mouth, Arthur saw me and he told Mrs. Kidd, the next thing I knew she was yanking me out of the chair. She said "so you want to steal food, well I fed you" she took the pan off the stove and told me to put my hand over the stove and hold it there, I remember I wouldn't do it she grabbed my hand and held it there, I was screaming and trying to get away she told Arthur to come help hold me I start screaming more she grabbed Castle and held her hand there also, I remember yelling and telling her that Castle didn't do anything.

The white man just kept on eating he never told her to stop or anything he just kept eating. I looked at him for help but he just looked away, when she was tired of fighting to hold us there she threw us in the floor and told us to get up and go to the bedroom and that she would be in there later I remember running to the room I looked back for Castle she was right behind me, when we got to the room I asked Castle why does she do these bad things to us, Castle just put her arms around me and said don't worry it will be alright and not to cry.

I told her that my hand was hurting so bad. My sister was always so attentive to me, she always showed me so much love and I loved her she was all I had in this world I needed her, she was my hope that no matter what happened to us we would come through it. My sister was a good, good person when we would get a beating I remember her saying to Mrs. Kidd while she was beating us, why are you doing this to us? We love you please stop, she would say this all the time, but I couldn't understand why she thought we loved this women.

She took my hand very gently in her hand and kissed it she told me that my hand would stop hurting soon because hers had stopped, I believed her and tried to quiet down but my hand just kept on hurting, later when I looked at my hand what I saw made me cry some more, my hand was all blistered up and swollen I held my hand with the other hand and prayed that everything would go away soon. It was dark and I just wanted to go to sleep so we both climbed into bed and covered up to go to sleep.

Chapter 5

The Other Room, the Pig and the Garden

THE NEXT DAY when we woke up I heard the white man talking, he was saying that he was going to bring a pig to Mrs. Kidd so that when the pig got big she could have the pig killed and that it would be food to eat. He told her that he was going to get the pig and would be back soon, it was at this point I realized that the man must live somewhere up the road, and that he must have spent the night with Mrs. Kidd.

It wasn't long that he left and Mrs. Kidd came in the room and told us to get up and come to her room I was afraid because after last night I wasn't sure what she was going to do to us, she was treating us worse every day. When we went to her room, she made us stand in a corner with our face to the wall. She told us that we were going to get a pig, and we had to make the pig a bed. She told us if we do a good job that she would give us something to eat, I think we might have thought this was good because we had not had any food for a while except what she had given in our hands to eat the night before. When we got outside we saw a pile of wood, I tried to lift a piece of the wood up, but it was so heavy, Castle tried too but we couldn't do it. She had given us some nails in our hands and a hammer, we really didn't know what to do or how to build this bed she wanted, but we bent down to try.

I remember we stayed out there a long time until almost dark, I remember telling Castle that we were going to get a beating because we had done a bad job of making a place for the pig to sleep. Arthur kept running in and out of the house telling Mrs. Kidd that we were not doing anything. After a while Mrs. Kidd came out to see what we had done, she yelled and yelled at us, she said that we had done nothing the whole time we had been outside and that the pig would be here soon, then she told us that we were not going to get anything to eat.

She yanked both of us up and told Arthur to bring one of the boards in the house, then she took us back to the room were we had slept the night before. She made us strip down to nothing, and then she stood us back to back and tied us together with a brown extension cord. By now Arthur had bought the piece of wood in the room, it had rusty nails in it, she started to beat us in the heads and all over our body with the nails going in and out of our bodies. She dared us not to fall; if we did, she told us the beating would last longer.

I remember it hurt so bad, we tried to hold our heads by ducking, but we couldn't, the dog skippy was right there biting us as she would say helping to beat us. This went on for a long time she kept saying that when she sends us to do something we had better do it right and that now the pig didn't have a bed and that the pig was important.

After she stopped beating us she threw us down on the bed still tied together and told us to figure out how to get a loose ourselves, I don't know how we did it but we managed to get ourselves a loose. We were bleeding from our heads, face legs and arms, Castle took the blanket on the bed and tried to wipe me up and I did the same for her. We cried for a long time while we tried to stop ourselves from bleeding, the pain was excruciating I can't explain how it felt to have nails going in and out of my body, but I don't wish this on anyone. As we sit there trying to stop the bleeding and the pain, we heard Mrs. Kidd outside of our window where the wood was that we tried to build a place for the pigs bed. I think that she was trying to make a bed for the pig to sleep, I could hear her voice and you could here some banging. It was dark outside by now and she was still out there, I knew as long as she was outside that she couldn't be beating on us. So we had a chance to just sit and catch our breath and try to stop hurting, When the banging stopped we became scared again, I remember talking to my sister about what we could do I asked did she think we should start planning on running away, she agreed with me, we thought it would have to be a day when she was not there but we had no idea when that would be, but that we would wait for that day.

The next day the white man bought the pig to the house, he called Mrs. Kidd out side to see the pig, she told him she didn't have much of a place for the pig to sleep. I didn't hear much after that because they stayed out back a while and then Arthur came and told us to come outside, when we got outside we saw the pig, he was in a little pen I guess the man had helped Mrs. Kidd build it, she told us that we had to feed the pig every day. After that I remember so many times being tied together butt naked with Castle and being beat with boards with nails in them I remember always wiping blood and finding anything to wrap our sores in, we were always getting beat for things and most of the time we didn't know why, she just thought of something and started to beat us, the dog was always right there with her when she began to beat us, this went on almost every day, we began to almost know when the beatings were going to happen. The day the pig came was when we found out what was behind the door in our room that had a lock and key on it.

After the white man had gone home and Mrs. Kidd and Arthur had eaten she came into our room with Arthur and gave us something to eat, she told us to hurry up and eat because she had a surprise for us. We wondered what the surprise could be, I wondered if it was going to be a good one or something we would have to do for her, I was scared and also curious because Mrs. Kidd was being nice to us so it seemed. When she left the room I asked Castle what did she think the surprise was, I don't think she knew what it was either, we just sit there and ate our food it wasn't a lot of food and we were afraid of what the surprise might be so we ate slow. Mrs. Kidd didn't come back right a way. When we had finished our food we just sat there and waited for the surprise.

When Mrs. Kidd and Arthur came back to the room I looked at her hands, she had four stockings in her hand and a key, she went to the door that was in our room and opened it, she told us to go in, when I looked around this room it was a bed in the left corner of the room I looked down at the floor the floor had spaces between each board they were far a part and it was very cold in the room, to the right was a tub it had legs on it she told us to take all our clothes off, then she took the stockings that she had in her hand and tied our hands behind our backs, then she put the stockings around our necks first me then Castle she told us to lay down on the floor with our heads near the legs of the tub, as we got down on our knees pieces of wood from the boards stuck in our knees and legs, she told us to lay on our backs, then she bent down and tied each one of us by our necks to the legs of the tub, she pulled the stockings real tight around our necks, almost choking us and then she left us there, her and Arthur and the dog just left us, we heard the door shut and I heard her lock it. I remember we started to scream and cry, we were so cold and scared I remember feeling things crawl all over my body, Castle told me to keep still because I was choking myself and that it was going to be ok. I just laid there and cried, I could hear Castle crying too, I was hoping that Mrs. Kidd would come back and let us out, but she never did, I asked Castle what did we do this time she said that she thinks it was because we didn't build the pigs a bed. Maybe what Castle said was true, I just couldn't figure out what the beating we had gotten not long ago was for.

I think we cried all night. That morning when it was day light I saw a snake in the corner curled up I thought that I had felt something like that crawl across me sometime earlier, Castle saw it to, she told me just to lay still that Mrs. Kidd should come and let us out soon, so I laid real still and prayed that she would come let us out.

A long time passed and the snake was still in the corner, then we heard the key in the door, the door opened and I saw the snake go down between one of the boards in the floor as she came in. Mrs. Kidd came over to us and bent down and untied us she told us to get up and go to the other room. It felt like I couldn't walk, but some how I made it to the bed. When I got to the bed I remember I felt so hungry I remember looking at the soap that was laying in the window I wondered how it would taste if I bite a piece, I picked up a piece and bit it, Castle asked me to give her some, we both ate the soap I don't know how much we ate, I just remember us eating some. As we sat there naked and cold we wondered if we could put our clothes on, we didn't know if we could or not so we just waited.

As I sat there thinking what we had went through the night before I began to think of my mother, I couldn't ever remember being treated this badly by her and I missed her, but I knew I would never see her again so I pushed back the tears and tried to get it out of my mind.

Mrs. Kidd came in a little while later and told us to put some clothes on and to come outside after we finish, when she had left the room I looked at Castle, she was crying I asked her why was she crying she told me that she felt sick I put my arms around her and this time I was the one saying that everything was going to be alright because God was going to take care of us.

Castle and I would always sing this song, I don't know where we learned it but we knew the words to it, as we tried to put our clothes on we started to sing "My eyes have seen the glory of the coming of the Lord he is tramping out the vineyards where the grapes of wrath are stored, he has loosed his faith of lightning of his terrible swift sword his truth is marching on glory, glory hallelujah glory, glory hallelujah glory, glory hallelujah his truth is marching on" about the time we had finished the verse Arthur came running in to let us no to get outside now, so we hurried and went outside, when we got outside, Mrs. Kidd pointed to out a big space near the back of the house near a well, It was nothing but weeds and sticks and these honeysuckle vines, she told us that we had to plant a garden and that we would have to dig it with our hands, Castle and I walked over to where she wanted us to start digging, we stooped down and began digging with our fingers we pulled on the vines that seemed to go on forever like there was no end, the ground was so hard and we kept pulling up rocks and weeds, Mrs. Kidd came over to where we were and gave us a couple of packages with seeds in them, she told us to plant it in the ground she said just dig a hole and put the seeds in the hole then get some water and pour in the hole. I remember it was so hard to dig the holes my hands started to bleed and so did Castle's but we kept digging and digging, we did this all day and most of the evening, from time to time Arthur would bring us out some water to drink, I remember hoping one of those times he would bring us something to eat anything would be nice, I started to feel sick. I think it was from the soap that we had eaten earlier.

We started to get very tired and the sun started to go down it started to get cool and we were cold and hungry, Arthur came out to get us and tell us to come in and that Mrs. Kidd said we could finish tomorrow, so we stopped and went inside, when we got inside Mrs. Kidd told us that in a few days the food we planted should come up and that we could eat it, at this time we didn't know any better then to think this was true, we soon found out that it was not true because when the food didn't come up we were put in the bathroom and tied up and beaten and left there under lock and key. This went on almost every day, if it wasn't the bathroom it was the tying us up naked back to back where she would beat us with the boards that had the nails in them until she and the dog got tired. Most of the time we would end up bleeding and barely able to walk a lot of times when she would finish and leave the room, we would just fall on the bed still tied up and stay there all night.

I remember some months must have passed because, it had started to be very cold outside, this one night she came into our room and woke us up, this time she gave us a sweater to put on and some socks she told us that the pig was dying and it needed food and that we had to help fix the food for the pig so that it would live. We put on the sweater and socks and went into the other room, it was very warm in this room and it felt good, Mrs. Kidd had started to cook some food for the pig she made us mix up some cornbread mix and peel some potatoes she had already cooked some chicken for the pig, I remember thinking that it must have been two or three days since we had anything to eat, I wondered why the pig got to eat and we didn't, we were so hungry, I remember Mrs. Kidd had this long plate and she filled it up with all the food she had cooked nothing was left at all on the stove or in the house it all went on the long plate for the pig.

After the plate was filled we all went outside except for Arthur, because he was sleeping, Mrs. Kidd carried the long plate outside, when we got to the pig he could barely stand up I remember Mrs. Kidd saying that we had to say a prayer for the pig I think she mumbled something and then she sat the food over into the pigs pen so the pig could eat, but the pig couldn't get up to eat. She told us that we would have to stand outside with the pig all night until he ate the food. At that point Mrs. Kidd went back into the house and we were left outside alone and cold and in the dark, it was so cold and icy outside my toes were very stiff. Castle told me that hers were too, I remember we hugged each other really tight and sang our song, we cried and hoped that the pig would eat, but it wouldn't it just laid there.

Mrs. Kidd came back out after a while and told us that she thinks the pig had died, so we just left the food there and went inside. When we got inside we went to our room, Mrs. Kidd followed us to the room she said in a very low voice that she hoped we didn't think that we were going to get away with killing the pig, that the white man had bought for her, she told us to strip down and stand there until she got back, I remember we were still so cold almost frozen, when she came back she had a extension cord with her and the dog, this time she didn't tie us together she just started to beat on us I think this was the worst beating of all, when your body is ice cold and someone takes a cord to it, the feeling is unbearable. I can't even explain to you what it feels like it is horrible and unforgettable the marks are still embedded in my body I see them every day.

I almost wish she had tied us together because if she had I would have never gotten an ugly scar one inch away from my temple, on the right side of my forehead. It will always be there to remind me of that terrible night. While she was beating us and the dog was biting us I fell and hit my head on the corner of the bed, blood was everywhere.

I jumped up and held my head with blood streaming down, when Mrs. Kidd saw this she stopped beating us and told me to sit on the bed, Castle was screaming and trying to get over to me, but Mrs. Kidd wouldn't let her. Mrs. Kidd went out of the room and came back with a white cloth she tied it around my forehead, but the blood kept coming out so she tied another one on top of that one, when the blood finally stopped a few hours later, I tried to take the white cloth off but when I tried it was stuck to my head and it hurt so I left it alone, Mrs. Kidd told me to leave it on and she would take it off later. I remember I never could take it off because it was stuck there. I wore it everyday and I never touched it.

Chapter 6

When We Ran Away

I REMEMBER ONE day the white man came to the house he said he was there to take Mrs. Kidd and Arthur and the dog away for a long while and that we would have to stay at the house by ourselves but only for a day or so. Mrs. Kidd said that we were to stay in the house while they were gone and that she would leave us something to eat. Well they all got into his car and they left, I think in one way it was a relief that they all were gone because we didn't have to worry about getting any beatings, but we were still afraid to stay in the house by ourselves, we looked around to find the food she had left for us to eat but never found anything.

I thought about what we should do, I asked Castle if she thought this would be a good time to run away, she said yes so we started to plan what we would do before Mrs. Kidd and Arthur and the white man came back. We decided that we would carry a blanket so we would have something to sit on if we got tired, there was nothing to eat so we thought that if we could just get to the big road with the lines on it that we could find something to eat from somewhere. I asked Castle was she scared, she said that she wasn't because anything was better than living here with Mrs. Kidd.

It was still real early in the day and we were anxious to get started, but we didn't want to leave to soon because we did not want Mrs. Kidd and the white man to see us in case they had not gotten far. We decided to wait a while before we left. I remember we kept looking out of the window to make sure that they were not going to come back to the house. After a good while we decided that it was safe and that they were gone and were not coming back.

We only had one fear and that was the church with the half horse, half man. When Mrs. Kidd would send us to the store which was a long, long way from the house, she would always tell us that if she sent us to the store and we didn't get back before dark that this thing would get us and tear our legs and arms off and that it would know when we pass because it could sense bad children when they were passing by. I remember sometimes she would send both of us and other times she just sent one of us, either way it was always nearing dark when we returned home, we had to carry a sack of cornmeal and a sack of potatoes it seemed like they were bigger then us and very heavy it was always a struggle to get it home. When ever we came to the church where the half horse half man was we stopped and stood for a bit and then we would run or walk as fast as we could depending on what we had in our hands to bring home, we decided that we would just have to do as we always have and that was to be brave and pray that we could make it pass and maybe it wouldn't see or hear us when we pass by.

We thought about it being time for us to get on the way and not waste time thinking about the church and that we would deal with it when we got there and just maybe it would not see us or hear us, so we put the blanket in the bag and we started out to see if there was a better place and better people in this world.

I started to feel free and feel like everything was going to be alright. As I looked over at Castle, she was smiling and walking very fast I had to run to keep up with her. When we got to the end of the road that we lived on, we stopped to make sure we didn't see Mrs. Kidd and the white man coming. As we ran down the road we started to sing, I wished that I could have ran faster but my legs hurt so bad and so did my head I still had the white cloth tied around my head where I had fell against the bed when Mrs. Kidd had been beating me, but I still kept up pretty good with Castle.

By now we were almost to the church where Mrs. Kidd said the monster was, as we approached the church we got very quiet and walked very softly but very fast pass the church we didn't look back we just kept going by, when we were safely pass the church we picked up our speed a little more. I remember saying to my sister that, it was a close call and I thought it would be nice never to walk pass it ever again or have to see it ever again. As we walked we were getting more hungry than ever I wondered if we would ever find food to eat. As we came up on another road we had to make a decision on what way to go, I looked down the road and saw some houses we thought it would be best to go that way because we would safe around more houses then in the open space. We turned to our left, the houses were not that close together but we felt safe. As we walked we saw some cows in a field. We stopped to look at them and then we came up on a white house with a white lady that had red hair. She was sitting on the porch in a rocking chair. I was afraid she would catch us and hold us if we said anything to her but I wanted to know how to get to a place were we would be safe from Mrs. Kidd. As we got closer to her house she stood up and watched us until we got there. When we were at the edge of her yard she spoke to us, I remember her speaking to us in a very nice voice saying, "Hello there you two and where are you going today?" I don't remember exactly what we said but I remember her asking us were we hungry, I do remember both of us saying yes.

She told us to sit down while she went in the house to get us something to eat and drink. I remember thinking that she was probably going in the house to call the police and tell them that she had found two little girls she thought were running away. I asked Castle what did she think and we decided that we would just go, when we got up to leave she came out of the house and asked us where were we going. She said that she was going to give us something to eat. In her hand she had two bowls and she gave them to us. It was the best tasting soup that we had ever had. I didn't want to eat to fast because I didn't want her to think that we were terribly hungry, but I couldn't help it.

Castle was eating very fast too, the lady went back in the house and when she came back she had a plate with crackers on it and cheese on top of the crackers, along with two glasses of milk. She told us to eat all we wanted and drink all of our milk. While we were eating, the lady asked what has happened to my head and I told her that I fell. I remember thinking that I was so full but I had to eat everything. When we had finished eating, almost everything was gone and she asked us how did we feel. Castle spoke up and told her that we had to go and she told us to wait a minute. When she came back out of the house she had two bottles of soda with her, and a bag.

In the bag was a sandwich cut in half and some more of the crackers with cheese on them. She said that it was nice to have met us and that if we just kept straight down the road we would come to a big, big road and that should take us where we wanted to go. I remember thinking that we didn't tell her where we wanted to go, she just pointed out where the big road was. As we gathered up our blanket and what she had given us to carry with us, I thought about how nice it would be to live with her. Castle pulled on me to go, so we said goodbye and we left.

I remember I started to get tired as we went on our way and wanted to lay down some where and get some sleep. Castle just wanted to keep on going so we did. We had walked a long while when a car came up behind us it was the first car we had seen that day, as the car got closer we stopped because it was so close behind us. When we stopped the car pulled beside us and my heart dropped, it was Mrs. Kidd and the white man. She got out of the car and yanked us in, she threw me first into the back seat as she slapped me in the back of the head and then she did the same to Castle. We were so shocked to see them. I wondered how she found us. I thought maybe the white lady that had fed us somehow had told them we had been at her house and that we were running away. There was nothing to say but sit in the back of the car and wonder what would happen when we get back to the house. I was so scared I could tell that Castle was too. Mrs. Kidd didn't say anything to us while we were in the car but Arthur kept laughing at us and telling us we were going to get it when we get home. Mrs. Kidd didn't say a word, to us but we could see that she was very mad. We heard her say to the man that she had ten dollars left at the house and that we had stole it and that we most have dropped it in that cow pasture back down the road, so that is where the white man took us back to. When we got there she got out and looked over the fence and came back to the car. She told him that the cows must have eaten it for grass. I heard the white man tell her that he would give her ten dollars. When he got back to the house, I just sat there and thought about how she was lying on us because we never saw any money the whole time we had been down here in that house.

When we got to the house, she told us to get out of the car and go in the house. As we were going to the house it started to snow. It looked so pretty coming down and it gave me a feeling of hope for some reason. I thought to myself that maybe she would be to busy with the white man and getting ready for the snow that she wouldn't think about punishing us for running away. I didn't want to go back into the bathroom and be tied to that tub any more. It was just to awful and scary. I thought I would just die if I had to go in there again. When we got inside the house we went straight to our room. Mrs. Kidd and the white man and Arthur stayed outside for a while. When I passed the window to go to our room I saw Arthur and the dog playing in the snow and I wished Castle and I could run and jump and play in the snow too. When we got to the room we just sat on the bed and wondered what would happen to us when she came in the house and when the white man would go home.

We heard Mrs. Kidd and Arthur and the dog come in the house. As I sat there, a funny feeling came over me. I started to feel like I didn't care anymore about what would happen to us. I knew something was going to happen, I just didn't know what and I didn't care. I felt that what ever was going to happen, it's going to happen. I didn't know what Castle was thinking at this time because we didn't say a word to each other she was just so quiet. She didn't even look at me and I didn't look at her. We just sat there waiting for what ever was going to happen. Even though I felt a since of calmness, I still feared what was about to happen to us. I thought this time, what ever she would do to us would be worst than any thing we had experienced so far. It was a long time that we sat there not knowing when she was going to come in and what she was going to do. I heard her tell Arthur to sit down and play with the dog and then she came in the room were we were. She stood there and looked at us for a bit then she said "You ran away and I told you to stay in the house. I thought you might do something like this that's why we decided to come back". She told us to stand up and take off our clothes and lay them on the bed. Then, she unlocked the bathroom door and told us to go in. When we got inside she took the stockings she had used before and tied our hands behind our back and shoved us down on our knees, first me and then Castle. When we were on our knees, she put a stocking around each of our necks and then she made us lie down on our backs while she tied each of us to the tub legs by our necks. After she finished tying us to the legs of the tub, she stood up and looked at us and said that we would have to stay in there for a long time for what we had done and then she left. I heard her lock the door from the other side and I wondered, how long was a long time?

Castle started to cry and so did I. We were so cold. I remember looking over in the corner and I could see the snow coming in through a hole in the ceiling. The floor where we lay with the boards were so far apart from each other and it was cold and muddy. I remember wishing that they had never found us and bought us back. I don't know how long we lay there, but I think it was about two days because I counted the nights and the days. We talked about how hungry we were and that we wished we had the food that the white lady had fed us when we had run away. We couldn't get a loose to go to the bath room and if we did we couldn't get out, and if we could, how would we get out back to go the bathroom? So we had to do it all over ourselves and we lay there in it. At the end of the second day when it had gotten dark, we heard the key turn in the lock. I knew it was Mrs. Kidd. I thought she was coming to get us and take us to the other room but I was wrong. When she came into the room, she had a brown extension cord with the one she always use to beat us with. She just started beating us with the cord and she kept saying that we somehow had untied ourselves and came through the locked door in the middle of the night and cut her hair off on one side of her head and went back into the room relocked the door from the outside and retied ourselves back up. I just lay there while she beat us. I couldn't move. I didn't have the strength and neither did Castle. We just lay there and cried. I remember looking up at her head as she was beating us, I could see what she was talking about. I saw that one side of her head did not have any hair. It was then that I closed my eyes and prayed that she would stop beating us soon. When she was tired of beating us she threw the cord down and left the room and locked the door.

We lay there cold and hungry in our urine and defecation with our bodies bloody and swollen. At that point, I wanted to die.

Chapter 7

Her Last Breath

THE NIGHT PASSED and the morning came. When we woke up I remember I felt like I was frozen and couldn't move. I asked Castle how she was and she said she felt the same way I did but that she was okay. I looked over to the corner where I had saw the snow coming in and saw a pile of snow on the floor it was a lot. I think we must have laid there most of the morning. When Mrs. Kidd unlocked the door and came in, she bent down and untied my neck and my hands. Then, she untied Castle and she was very quiet and didn't say a word to us. She went back out of the room and when she came back she told Castle to get in the tub. While she went out to the well and get some water to pour on her, because she stunk, she looked at me and said, "After I finished with her, you are next." It took everything Castle had to put her legs over the side of the tub to get in and everything I had to help her, as I was helping her she put her arms around my neck and held on as tight as she could she said me. "I Love you Myra and we are going to be alright. I love Mrs. Kidd too. I don't know why she doesn't love us, but I love her." She fell over into the tub. She held my hands very tightly. Now as I look back to that day I know that she was trying to let me know that she was tired. She tried to be strong for me, then without any help at all she stood up straight and tall in the bathtub.

I looked at her with tears running down her cheeks as she stood there and waited for whatever was going to happen to her. She didn't seem afraid and she just stood there with her head looking up to the ceiling. I wondered what she was looking at. When I looked up, all I saw was the ceiling. A few minutes passed, Mrs. Kidd was back. In her hand she was carrying a bucket of water. She walked over to Castle and lifted the bucket of water and poured it over her head very fast. The sound that came out of Castle was horrifying. Mrs. Kidd looked at me as she was leaving the room and said, "You are next so be in the tub when I get back".

She left the door open behind her. I turned to see if Castle was alright. She looked okay but was just standing there. A few minutes later, she fell out of the tub and into my arms, I caught her. Then she looked up at me and said, "I love you, Myra". I remember she was heavy for me to hold so I dragged her to the wall. As I was dragging her, I saw a bowel movement come out of her and then I just fell up against the wall and slid down to the floor. Castle fell with me and landed on top of me. I tried to wake her up before Mrs. Kidd got back but she wouldn't wake up. I tried to move her off of me but I couldn't. I told her that if she didn't wake up now, we were going to get in more trouble but she just kept on sleeping so I just sat there with her laying in my arms. I started to rock her and sing to her. I guess I knew something more was wrong.

Mrs. Kidd came in she had another bucket of water with her. She looked over at me holding Castle and sat the water down on the floor. She came over to us and I was crying. I told her that Castle wouldn't wake up and that I had been trying very hard to wake her up but she wouldn't. She took Castle from me and carried her to the bed, laid her in it and covered her up. I asked her what was wrong with her and she said that Castle was in something that made her look like she was dead but she was only sleeping and when she finished resting she would wake up.

I remember being relieved that Castle would wake up soon. Mrs. Kidd told me that we would wait for a day or so for Castle to wake up and that if she didn't, she would go get someone to wake her up. I believed what she said. She brought me into the living room and sat me on the couch. She gave me some food and something to drink. I didn't want much to eat because I wasn't that hungry and I wanted to save some for Castle when she woke up. Mrs. Kidd asked me why I wasn't eating my food and I told her that I wanted to save some for Castle and wait for her to eat with me. Mrs. Kidd said that it would be enough for Castle and that I could eat my food. I tried but I couldn't bring my hands to my mouth and for some reason I couldn't move my legs. I remember we sat up most of the night. Arthur and the dog didn't bother me. We just sat in that room all together and said nothing. I kept watching the door were Castle was sleeping and thinking she would be coming in the room were we were anytime but she didn't come. I thought to myself, "I will just wait until she comes out of the room were she was sleeping."

When the morning came, Mrs. Kidd got up and went into the room where Castle was. When she came back out she said that Castle had not woke up yet and that she would have to walk up the road to call someone to help wake her up. Before she left she went into the room where Castle was and did her hair. Then, she put on her coat and took the stockings she had tied us up with and put them in her coat pocket. Then she looked at me and Arthur and said that when the people and her get back, this is what we should always remember to say because where ever we go she could always see us and that she would always find us. If we told anything different than what she had told us to say, she would know it and that she would come and kill us so just say only what she said to say.

Chapter 8

The Murder Untold

SHE TOLD US to say to the people that would come to get Castle, that we had been out playing in the snow. We had climbed up a ladder to the roof and that Castle had fallen off and broke her neck. But I know there was no ladder and we had never been on the roof. We couldn't even walk. And except for going to the store, Castle and I were never apart. I remember thinking that I should say everything she said to say because I didn't want her to kill me or Arthur. Then she left, I looked out of the window and watched her until she was out of sight.

Mrs. Kidd was gone a very long time. All I wanted to do was go in the next room and wake Castle up but when I tried to do that I couldn't walk so I just waited for Mrs. Kidd to get back. After a while I saw her come back, she came in the house and told us, "The police are coming and would be here soon". She then told us that she had taken the stockings with her and threw them away, because Castle had marks on her neck from playing with them. She said that was what we should say if the police ask anything about the marks on Castle neck.

I never remember any marks on Castle's neck. I guess I didn't see them but I knew if there was any marks, it came from when she would tie us by our necks in the bathroom to the tub. I was very afraid of Mrs. Kidd so any thing she said to say I thought it best to do so. I said okay at this point. I don't think I understood what was going on. It wasn't long when I looked out of the window and saw two police cars and an ambulance in the yard. Mrs. Kidd went outside to talk with the police. While she was with the police, two men from the ambulance came in the house. They stopped and asked me were was my sister sleeping. I pointed to the room where she was. One of men stayed with me and the other went on to where Castle was. The man started to talk to me and as he was talking, he touched my arms and legs and asked how did I feel. I told him I didn't feel good he told me he was going to take me to the hospital so that I would feel better. He then asked me did I want to walk or did I want him to carry me. I said that I would walk but when I tried I started to fall. The ambulance man caught me and picked me up. The other man came out of the room where Castle was and kept pass me and the man holding me. When we got outside he put me in the ambulance in a bed he left the door open. I could see the policeman talking to Mrs. Kidd. She was pointing to the top of the house and then I heard one of the policemen ask her did she see my eyes. She turned and pointed to the top of the house. The policeman pulled Mrs. Kidd to the ambulance where I was laying and said "Did you see her eyes?" Once again, Mrs. Kidd pointed to the top of the house then the policeman shoved her up against this big tree in the front yard and said to her, "I asked you did you see her black eyes?" She told him no. It was then that I knew I had two black eyes and I wondered what I looked like. I reached up to touch my head where the rag was and also found out I had no hair on my head.

I asked the ambulance man was he going to bring Castle with us and he said that she was coming later. He said that I am safe now and that I should lie down and rest. He closed the door of the ambulance and got in the front seat of the ambulance and started to drive down the dirt road. As I looked out of the back of the ambulance I saw the policeman still talking to Mrs. Kidd. When we got out on the road, I saw a long black car pass us and turn on the road where we stayed. I knew the car was coming for Castle and I thought to myself, now she will be safe too. I thought about all the things Mrs. Kidd said to say. I knew the things Mrs. Kidd had said to say was not true but I didn't know if she had the power to know when I would tell the true story so I kept the truth to myself and only a selected few knew what I knew. 43 years later, I can tell the story exactly the way it was.

Chapter 9

I Survived

ACCORDING TO THE case file that I recently had a chance to view, I was taken to Mary Washington Hospital in Fredericksburg, VA. I remember when I arrived, a man in a white coat came over to me and he looked at my head wrapped up in the bloody rag, as he talked to me he started to pull on the rag and said, "Tell me sweetie, did someone beat you up?" And at that moment he yanked the bloody rag from my head. I remember screaming very, very loud and the next thing I remember was waking up in another room where the doctor was showing me my x-rays. He told me to look at them. Along with the two black eyes I also had two broken legs, two broken arms and it seemed that every inch of my body hurt to the touch and it hurt to move. The next thing I remember I was in a different ambulance and I was going down a long, long road again.

I remember learning that Castle had died through one of the nurses at the hospital and I remember her holding me all night while I cried for my sister. I wanted her to be safe like I was now, but in all aspects she was better off than I was. She was safe in the arms of God; He took her home with him.

According to the case file I was shipped off to MCV Hospital in Richmond, VA., and placed in protective custody and my name was changed. After three years, my name was changed back to Myra. I was taken out of protective custody and returned back to Spotsylvania County.

The case file said that Mrs. Kidd had been tried and found guilty and was sent to Petersburg Va. For Six months and then was released. She would be 81 yrs. old now and I often wonder did her mind catch up with her for what she did to us.

The case files said that we were brutally beaten, I think brutally is an understatement. The news paper articles didn't say she was punished for my sister's death, just that she was punished for neglect, but it was the neglect and primitive conditions that we lived in and the brutal beatings that we endured during this time that resulted in A Murder Untold.

The next few pages show some news clippings in relation to my sister's death/murder.

14 The Free Lance-Star, Fredericksburg, Virginia
Monday, February 1, 1965

Death of Child, Injury Of Second Are Probed

The Spotsylvania Sheriff's Department is investigating the death of one child and injury of another at a location near Margo.

Found dead in a bed at the home yesterday was Castle Lewis, a 9-year-old Negro girl. Taken to Mary Washington Hospital by the Rescue Squad and later transferred to a Richmond hospital with a leg injury was Myra Crutchfield, 10.

Deputy Sheriff Ralph Johnson said the two children were living at the home of Eunice Kidd.

Complete Course

QUANTICO — Civilian employe supervisors in the Marine Corps Schools' Guadalcanal area have completed an advanced supervisory development training conducted here by O. R. Whitelock, employment development officer.

He said both children are from Washington and that the Kidd woman—also from Washington—was apparently keeping them for their mother.

Johnson quoted the Kidd woman as saying the two children apparently fell from a roof of the one-story home some time Saturday. She said she put the Lewis child in bed after the fall and called the sheriff's office Sunday when the child did not wake up.

The body of the dead child has been sent to the chief state medical examiner's office in Richmond for an autopsy and Johnson said an investigation of the case is continuing.

Sheriff B. W. Davis Jr. said that the Margo home was little more than a shack and said that living conditions there were primitive. He said the bed in which the dead child was found was located near toilet fixtures.

F.S. Feb. 9, 1965

Obituaries

CASTLE LEWIS

A graveside service for Castle Lewis, 9, of Spotsylvania County will be held Wednesday at 1 p.m. at St. Paul Baptist Church Cemetery, Margo. The procession will leave Kay & Silkey Funeral Home at 12 noon.

The child died Jan. 31 of injuries received at her home.

FLS
Feb. 10, 1965

Mental Tests Are Ordered For Woman

A mental examination at Central State Hospital in Petersburg was ordered yesterday for a Spotsylvania County woman charged with child neglect.

Juvenile and Domestic Relations Judge Francis B. Gouldman ordered the examination for Mrs. Eunice Kidd, 38, of near Margo.

She is charged by the county sheriff's department with neglect of a 10-year-old child in her custody. The child, Myra Crutchfield, is hospitalized in Richmond with injuries of the legs and feet.

Another child in the woman's custody, Castle Lewis, 9, died in late January of a brain concussion, apparently suffered in a fall from a roof at the Margo home.

A third child—a 6-year-old boy—was removed from the woman's custody and turned over to the county Welfare Department.

Medical Examiner Issues Report In Girl's Death

The death of a 9-year-old Negro girl at a location near Margo in Spotsylvania County has been attributed to a brain concussion, in a report filed by the chief state medical examiner's office.

Dr. W. H. Johnson, Spotsylvania medical examiner, said a final autopsy report from the state office revealed the child, Castle Lewis, showed some signs of malnutrition and neglect, but not enough to contribute to her death.

He said also that one of the state examiners had questioned a second child involved, Myra Crutchfield, 10, who is hospitalized in Richmond and that the child had corroborated a story told by Eunice Kidd who was keeping the children for their mother.

The child was quoted as saying that she and the Lewis girl —her sister—fell while climbing a crude ladder outside the small home at Margo last Saturday evening.

After the fall, the Crutchfield girl was quoted as saying, she went in the house and laid down until Mrs. Kidd asked the whereabouts of her sister. When informed about the fall, Mrs. Kidd went outside and found the Lewis child semi-conscious. She brought her into the house, put her to bed and sat up with her all night, according to the Crutchfield girl.

On Sunday morning when the Lewis girl could not be awakened, Mr. Kidd called the sheriff's department, according to the Crutchfield girl.

The Fredericksburg Rescue Squad took the surviving girl to Mary Washington Hospital and she was transferred to the Richmond hospital suffering from injuries to the legs and feet.

Neglect Charge Placed Against Margo Woman

A warrant charging neglect of a child in her custody has been issued against Mrs. Eunice Kidd of near Margo in Spotsylvania County.

The warrant alleges that Mrs. Kidd showed neglect in the care of Myra Crutchfield, 10, who is now hospitalized in Richmond with injuries of the legs and feet.

The Crutchfield girl was hospitalized last Sunday at the same time that her sister, Castle Lewis, 9, was found dead at the Margo home. A medical examiner's report showed that the Lewis girl died of a brain concussion, apparently suffered in a fall. The report said further the dead child showed evidence of malnutrition and neglect but not enough to contribute to her death.

Spotsylvania authorities also announced that a 6-year-old boy in Mrs. Kidd's care has been turned over to custody of the Spotsylvania Welfare Department. They said Mrs. Kidd concurred in the action.

A hearing for Mrs. Kidd on the neglect charge is tentatively set for Tuesday in the Spotsylvania Juvenile and Domestic Relations Court.

After the incident, my mother had started to look and had been trying to prepare a place for me but unfortunately, she never found one. It came to my knowledge that she had been searching for me for about 2 yrs. but eventually ceased on doing so. Here are the letters that my mother had written from the time that she had been trying to locate me.

Due to the nature of this book, it is my belief that some of the facts in the letters have been altered or changed recently.

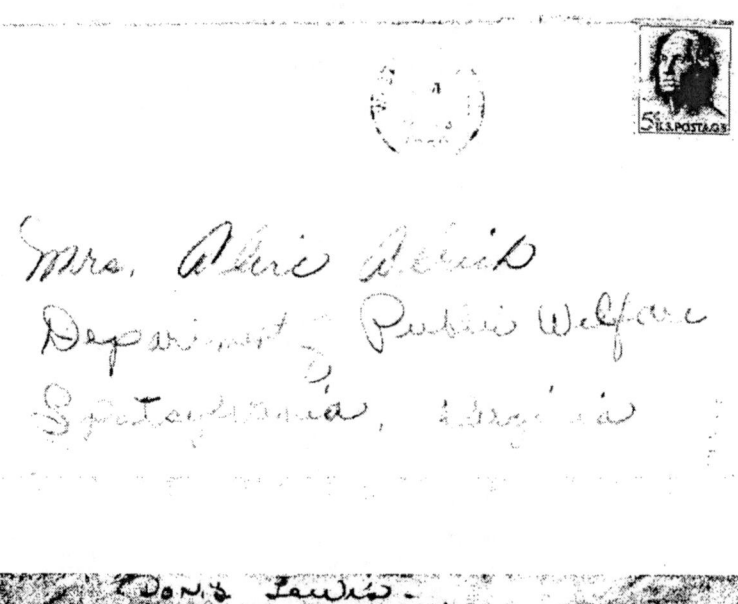

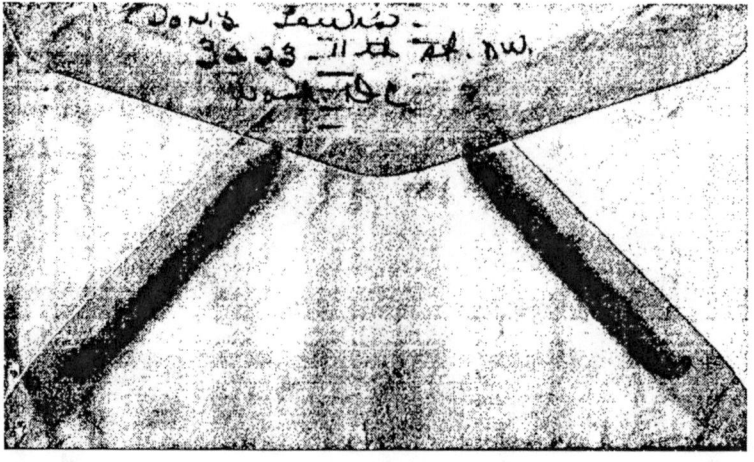

April 23, 1965
223 - 1st St. NW.
Washington, DC
Basement Apartment

Mrs. Aldrich,

I've been waiting word from you or someone from the department there. And I haven't heard any word as to Myra's condition or if I can come visit her or any word at all. I've called Sheriff Davis a couple of times and he's told me to contact you, but I can't keep calling from my job and when I get home the office is closed.

I took a day off from work to go to the welfare department here as far as I know I can bring her home as soon as I get a larger apartment well I'm getting a larger apartment in a house the first week in May, but I do think I should see Myra and that she should be prepared for the fact that her mother will and is making plans for to be returned to her. I haven't been told as to what has happen about the trail of Mrs Kidd, I don't know what the charges are for her if I should obtain a lawyer or not. I spoke to an attorney and he wanted to know what the charges were and if I needed a lawyer before he went any further, but I've been waiting word from your department. I've made most of the necessary arrangements as for my son coming home except for getting the place, that will be taken care of next month. If it's necessary you can call me in the evening after 6:30 pm and reverse the charges just so I know how the child is doing and when and what I'm to do. It's very difficult for me because I'm here in the District and she's there, the only thing I can do is call or write. So I rely on the department to call me or write me because I'm at work all day and I just can't make long distance calls from my job because this phone is limited and there's very important calls always coming in on this phone

I'm at work from 8am until 5:30 pm home at 6:30 pm so you can reach me at work at this number 589-6864 or home at 483-6185. Please let me hear from you. The middle part of May I'll be taking classes after 7:30 pm for a Medical Assistance Course so I'd like to hear from you as soon as possible. I do want to thank you once again for all you've done.

Thank you,
Mrs. Doris Lewis

May 26, 1966
4002 -4th Street S.E. #202
Washington, D.C. 20032

Mrs. Alice Alrich,
Re: Myra Crutchfield

Mrs. Alrich,
    I have tried to get some information about visiting my child Myra, and as of today there has been no respond to my request for such permission. I've tried waiting for a reply from the welfare department here and they not contacted me in no way as to if this would be possible. The only thing that was told to me was that there was no reason for my not seeing her if your department knew of the day of the visit. Since then they were to contact you for such information.
    Mrs. Harris has left the agency and there is some one filling her place and that person was to contact me and no such transaction has been made. So I've decided that the best thing to do was to contact you.
    Some time ago you sent me a letter telling me that it was not wise for Myra to be moved until the end of the school term in June of this year. I've been very concern about her coming home. If Myra still feels that she doesn't want to return home with the other part of her family I'd still like to see her anyway. My home life has changed in some respects but the welfare department here has not visit heresince Mrs. Harris left the agency and she was to send a letter to your department to that efect. I'd like very much to here from you concerning the possiblty of Myra's coming home the end of the school term. I'm now free during the day for a week or more so if a visit is needed during the next five or six days I'll make the nessary arangements. Please forward this information to me as soon as possible. I wonder has any one told Myra how much her mother and her sister and brother would like to have her home with us again, she proabley thinks we really aren't concerned if this has not been told to her. We have tried very hard to get this to happen but it seems there has always been some reason as to why she could not return home the reasons my may have been valid but they haven't always seemed that to me. I'll never understand how anyone can prevent a mother from seeing her child unless she has been proven an unfit mother and no such evendence has been stated against me. Visiting rights has been always permitted unless the child has been adopted and no such transactions has been made to my knowledge. Thes facts were pointed out to me from a legal persons point.

                Thank you,
                Mrs. Doris Lewis

FEB 18 1965   3223-11 26 St. N.W.
Washington, D.C.

Dear Mrs Alkins,

I know that you are doing everything possible to let me know about my child Myra, I do believe this anyway. I know that I showed at the time I saw you, showed a little emotion but I couldn't. It's not that I didn't love Castle very much I know that this is a very poor way of showing it but Mrs Kidd could have let me know of the condition of the care of the children and I would have gladly came forth and did my best or I would have taken those children back but I told her when and if she decided to go to rea [?] or she had told me the way I'd come down brought things and even take them on week ends and bring them back then she spelled too because if they were in her care she told me she would not me to take them off for no week ends since we had signed this agreement though a notary Public. So this I tried to understand even though I didn't realy like the idea but the kids seemed very happy. I can't understand why she told you at the [hifuuels?] there that she could [desert?] me. Before she had the children I was in PA and when she had them I had my checks sent to her Home & I [cashed?] those checks and gave her from $125.00 to [?] [?] [Kids home?] from Sept of 63 until I had them stopped in Sep of 64, we both agreed because I had trouble getting my case work to send them out or to my Case worker even smiled [?] in [Mrs.?] Kids Home then and talked with the two girls,

Her name is Miss Mary D—
I even paid full fee for two out
of my checks, if she had wanted
to. She could have called that
worker or else sent her a letter.
Also she would have contacted
me or my family even if the
case was closed they still
had all information of me and
my family in the files. There
But there's only been her side
of the story, but I'll do everything in my power to get Myra
back and try to make forget some
of the pain she has suffered
for the last nine months. As
for Calvin, he believed me
your personal reasons because
I had told him one night to
keep him in his place.

There is a fellow she used to go with besides Kelly that was there quite often because I go there evenings and we'd all play cards and I enjoyed going there because I'd see the children and I could spend as much time as I liked. I'm trying to get the information you like but I'm up a dead end street I'm just by myself. I'm planning the case & trying to put myself in the hands of a lawyer as a fact I'm trying to — let's put it that way in case I need help in obtaining her back now. Maybe when the hearing comes up he'll be there and maybe not all depends on what he thinks my chances are if he feels he can do some good then I'll have to know when

I come. I'm off this Monday because of a holiday for the people where I work. So that is a day I'd like to come home discuss this more fully and possibly see Myra if you can arrange this. So call me at home Saturday morning or on the job Friday before 4 P.M. If that's possible I'll bring as much information as possible for you then. I'd feel a lot better if I could talk this thing out and possibly see Myra or talk to the judge on Monday. My mind wasn't at all clear on Sunday. In the first week of May I'll be finish my course in typing & shorthand and I'll have a decent job and income and be capable of caring

dear Myra properly. Like I
was doing so I could bring
[back] to their home, but maybe
I wanted to long at least for
Castle sake anyway now I
can [...] with the men I
have left Anyway give [...]
[...] the Sheriff and the
persons you all the help you
have given me and all that you
will do in the future.
Please call me,

        Mrs. [Dawn Lewis]

P.S. This letter is probably hard
to read but I'm at work and
holding the baby so you can
understand.

Author's Note

THINGS HAVE NEVER been the same after what had happened. What you have read is just a part of the chapters in my life and it was not easy for me to relive these dreadful memories. Yet, I thank God that I have found the courage to share these with you.

We all go through terrible things sometimes, but if you can come out of them alive and still have your sanity and know who to thank for this, what a strong, strong person you have become. I survived a murder untold and will always know who to thank and praise.

It's been forty-three years and I never could write this story, I have tried so long. But thanks to God who strengthens me and all the loving people around me. My heart and my mind have survived to tell it, and now I'm healing.

As I carry on with this venture, I am thankful for all of your support and I pray that my books will reach out and inspire you in some way.

This Is Dedicated To The One I Love

DID YOU KNOW that God above created you and me for each other to love? He picked us out from all the rest, because he knew we'd need each other to nest

I love you Castle from my heart, I never thought we'd be apart You were so amazing how you took care of me; I knew you knew I'd be the one to tell this story.

I am so sorry it took me so long to write what is true, but I was waiting for God to give me the cue. I was trying to heal from the scars and the pain; I carried you with me so I could stay sane.

What we went through God had our backs, he knew I would remember and one day tell the true facts.

I remember how you loved me with your heart and your soul, God has you with him now to have and to hold.

I found out after forty-three years where your body is lying, I'm coming to visit and finish crying.

I want to place flowers on your grave with love and give all praises to God above; this is dedicated to the one I will always love

To My Sister Castle,
From your sister, Myra.